What This Book Will Do for You

By the time you finish reading this book, you'll feel more comfortable assigning work you might have done yourself to someone else. You'll see how using delegation as a management tool helps you as a supervisor to achieve your objectives, those of your work groups or teams, and those of the organization, while helping your employees to grow.

D0684877

Other Titles in the Successful Office Skills Series

HOW TO
DELEGATE
Effect-
ively →

Donald H. Weiss

amacom
American Management Association

This book is available at a special
discount when ordered in bulk quantities.
For information, contact Special Sales Department,
AMACOM, a division of
American Management Association
135 West 50th Street, New York, NY 10020.

Library of Congress Cataloging-in-Publication Data

Weiss, Donald H., 1936–
    How to delegate effectively.

    (The Successful office skills series)
    Includes index.
    1. Delegation of authority. I. Title. II. Series.
HD50.W45   1988   658.4'02   88-47697
ISBN 0-8144-7700-3

Printing number

10 9 8 7 6 5 4 3 2 1

CONTENTS

Introduction:

Why Delegating Is So Important

Ask Roxanne Fischer why she's working late, and she'll lament:

> Too much trivia during the day. I can't get anything *important* done. Clerical tasks! Just look at all these reports. And helping everyone, explaining how to do things. How do they expect me to manage this unit?

So why doesn't she get help from her employees?

> I've keyed in these training manuals for twelve years. No one can do it better than I. Anyone I give it to is sure to blow it, and my backside'd be in a sling. I'd better do it myself. Besides, it's my job. If I give it away, what'll I do? Oh well, another night of staying late. Either I do it myself or it won't get done.

What's that? You've heard others say those things, and perhaps you've even said them yourself?

If so, you're making your own life difficult through poorly defined goals and objectives, badly organized calendars, and inadequately distributed work. In turn, your subordinates suffer because their interests as well as their talents are overlooked, however unintentionally. In short, by not delegating, you fail to make effective use of all your resources, both material *and* human.

By the time you finish reading this book, you'll learn the hard lesson that Roxanne Fischer and many supervisors need to learn: how to give away *non*supervisory work and how to get help from other people. You'll feel more comfortable assigning work you might have done yourself to someone else, and you'll see that using delegation as a management tool helps you to achieve your objectives, those of your work group or team, and those of the organization, while helping your employees to grow.

Chapter 1

How to Separate Your Objectives From Those of Your Work Unit

In a nutshell: *Supervisors see to it that the unit accomplishes its objectives;* that's what "getting positive results" means. That's a supervisory objective, not a mission objective.

A unit's work objectives and supervisory objectives are not one and the same. A work unit's objective—getting positive results—directs the unit's *mission,* for which line employees are responsible. That could involve making something from raw materials or completing projects that satisfy organizational objectives or providing services to consumers or support services that help other units do their work.

Supervisory objectives involve getting those results by hiring, training, coaching, counseling, and directing other people; by planning, problem solving, monitoring, taking corrective action, and rewarding for success. A supervisor doesn't have to get results by doing the unit's work.

Sure, in the real world, some management schemes require supervisors to perform the same kinds of tasks their employees do: *mission work.* Such people are called working supervisors. And, by setting high individual production goals for them, management often makes the mission work more important than the supervisory work. The supervisor then struggles to take off one hat and don the other—or, even to find the time to try.

[*If you count yourself among the number of working*

3

Unit vs. Supervisory Objectives

Unit objective: Getting positive results, the work for which line employees are responsible

Supervisory objectives: Getting results by hiring, training, coaching, counseling, directing, planning, problem solving, monitoring, taking corrective action, rewarding

---

supervisors, don't rush off to give away your mission work before checking with management about what you can or can't delegate, to whom you can or can't delegate, when you can or can't delegate. You're a working supervisor because management wants it that way. Mess around with your organization's practices without checking out the limits of your authority and you may find yourself supervising somewhere else.]

When You Battle With Delegating

This book is for supervisors who have the *right* to delegate but have problems balancing group objectives with their own, giving up their responsibilities, or assigning work they otherwise would do. We're talking to the Roxannes of the world: working supervisors who have the right to delegate work but who don't exercise it or who exercise ineffectively.

Did you notice how many times Roxanne used "I," "me," "my," or "myself"—first-person personal pronouns? Go back and count them.

Come up with thirteen? In relation to her total number of words, that's a lot of "me, myself, and I"—nearly 13 percent.

Supervisors who have difficulty delegating usually use first-person pronouns too often. Although the unit objectives for which they are responsible belong to the work group as a whole, they take on too much mission work for themselves instead of balancing the group's

4

objectives and their own against each other. Later, you'll learn to separate the two and establish priorities between them.

The best technicians, you see, don't always make the best supervisors. They need help to come out of their comfort zone and adopt management rather than line-employee attitudes—as in the case of Roxanne, who thinks that by delegating, she's *giving up* her responsibilities. Like many managers, she feels more comfortable doing the work that got her to where she is than assuming the supervisory duties that threaten her. Even people with supervisory training sometimes use their mission work to put off or put aside their supervisory duties.

Roxanne also feels that she's not making an "appropriate contribution" unless she's doing mission work. She sees management duties as "trivial," largely a matter of "shuffling paper and dealing with bothersome people." Like many others, she feels that that's not "real work."

But those aren't Roxanne's only problems. No, she's one of those supervisors who won't give up a large piece of the work (in her case, producing training manuals and other major manuscripts) because she doesn't think anyone can do it as well as she can. Naturally, she's never assigned it to anyone so she can't know if she's right or wrong.

Of course, she may not *want* to know. She could be threatened, as many supervisors are, by the possibility that someone else can do the work at least as well as she can. Then, as she queried, what would she do?

Supervise more. Roxanne's supervisory duties often don't get done or are hurriedly fulfilled, and the unit's productivity suffers. She doesn't understand that when she gives up mission work, she doesn't give up responsibility. Management is real work with its own responsibilities, and delegating happens to be an important management responsibility. Let's see how that works.

The decision-making group—the board of directors, the ownership, the partnership, whatever it is in your organization—confers its authority to run the company

Exhibit 1. The flow of authority and responsibility.

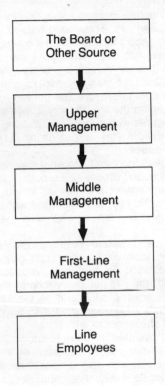

on upper management. Upper management confers some of its authority on you, wherever you are in the organization, by passing some of its responsibilities through middle management.

The pass-through takes place when the middle managers confer a range of authority and assign responsibility for unit objectives on line supervisors, who see to it that the units achieve their goals—goals that contribute to achieving organizational goals. That doesn't mean that supervisors have to do the mission work themselves, unless upper management says they must.

Your authority, as it finally comes down to you, includes your right to decide how to organize and use your resources in whatever manner best accomplishes the unit's objectives. When you delegate, you pass your authority to do a job or accomplish an objective to an employee or to another person in a work group who reports to you. You assign temporary work the other person *would not ordinarily do* (by virtue of the role assigned to him or her by the job description) *that you would have had to do yourself*. You then hold that person accountable for its successful completion.

Look at Exhibit 1, which diagrams the flow of authority and responsibilities just outlined. Chapter 2 explains how authority and responsibility add up to accountability.

Chapter 2

Authority + Responsibility = Accountability

A supervisor delegates work within the context of his or her range of authority and span of responsibility. Those produce the supervisor's accountabilities: the results people expect from him or her.

When you give a person responsibility and the authority to carry it out, you expect the person to meet the goals in the prescribed period of time. That expectation is what we mean by accountability.

Roxanne supervises a word processing unit in a medium-size insurance company. Eight people (called word processors, not typists) report to her. Her span of responsibility, range of authority, and accountabilities extend over the work that she and the eight employees produce and the way in which they produce it.

If she worked alone in her unit, her authority would be limited to carrying out the responsibilities of a word processing job. She could decide how best to get the work done, and that's about it. The work defines the worker's authority and responsibilities.

Any position consists of a set of responsibilities (tasks or duties) that the person occupying the position is expected to achieve. They're objectives or goals of the position, and they dictate what activities the person should do, the means he or she should use, and the conditions under which he or she will work to achieve those goals or objectives. Those goals and activities, taken all together, are called a span of responsibility. With responsibility usually goes the authority to carry it out properly.

Your authority consists of the right and the power to make and follow through on decisions. Every job involves making decisions, although at times it seems as if you have no authority at all; somebody seems to make the decisions for you. However, your range of authority consists of the objectives over which you exercise your right and power.

That range of authority could be very narrow, as in the case of doing the work of the unit. A line employee's authority usually extends no further than deciding *when* to perform specific activities, although sometimes that authority extends to deciding on the means (but not always), in which case, his or her authority also covers *how* the job is performed.

Your range of authority, as supervisor, extends much further than that. Although it may not always seem as if you make any decisions, you probably do: who's to do the work; how the work's to be done; how well the work is being done; when to take corrective action; when to reward for work well done; when, to whom, and how to delegate work. The decisions you make about the responsibilities in your work unit define the limits of your accountabilities.

Accountability refers to the outcomes a worker is expected to produce and the standards by which they're measured. For example, in Roxanne's unit, one word processor is expected to produce 30 one-page letters a day with no errors. Roxanne holds the person accountable for doing that job. She takes corrective action when he or she doesn't fulfill that responsibility, or she rewards the word processor for doing the job well.

Accountabilities imply the consequences of success or failure: what happens when the job is completed or if it isn't. When assigning or delegating work, you spell out the positive or negative consequences *to the worker*, and you also spell out how success or failure affects other people in the unit, the unit's objectives, and the organization's goals. What would happen if the word processor pumped out only 20 one-page letters? Consider, if you will, the ripple effect.

You can delegate any responsibility to anyone who

reports to you as long as it fits with the demands of the unit's mission. The delegation also has to fit with the person's ability to do the job or to learn how to do it in a reasonable amount of time. With the responsibility, you have to delegate the authority appropriate for carrying it out. You also have to set the standards of accountability.

But before you can delegate a job effectively, you must have a clear and unambiguous idea of the nature of the task and the activities required for doing it. You need a task analysis.

Task Analysis

Does your organization have a description of every position, including yours (as supervisor)? Those descriptions should outline what the positions are supposed to accomplish; the jobs or tasks are the responsibilities that go along with the position. The descriptions should identify the objectives—the outcomes—expected of anyone occupying that position and then list the ordinary activities required to achieve them. That way, the description spells out the position's full span of responsibility.

A delegated task is not included in the span of a person's ordinary responsibilities. It is her or his responsibility only for however long the employee is required to do or complete the task. That responsibility is either in *your* job description or assigned to your unit in addition to its ordinary responsibilities. This section discusses only responsibilities in your job description.

Of course, this assumes you have a list that separates your supervisory responsibilities from your line responsibilities. Let's take Roxanne's position. Although she doesn't realize it, the range of her authority extends to designing and redesigning job descriptions as long as what she does conforms to the mission of the unit. First, she needs a mission statement to know exactly how to proceed. Let's write one for her.

Prepare for mailing all company correspondence for everyone but department heads with secre-

Delegated tasks are not included in the span of a person's ordinary responsibilities. They are temporary unless assigned permanently as part of the job description.

----

taries; prepare all small-volume publication materials not sent for printing; periodically, and as needed, prepare any other printed matter assigned that is not ordinarily assigned to the unit.

That statement spells out all the objectives of Roxanne's unit. The wording of the statement leaves no doubt about the work the group's supposed to do.

First, it's *action-oriented*. The mission is expressed through action verbs: "prepare," "sent for printing."

Next, it's *specific*. It refers to the kinds of work on which word processors take action: "*all* company *correspondence* for mailing for everyone but department heads with secretaries"; "*all small-volume publication materials. . . .*"

Still, it does have a less-than-specific catchall clause: "periodically, and as needed, prepare any other printed matter assigned that is not ordinarily assigned to the unit." But even that has some limiting traits: "periodically, and as needed, . . . prepare . . . printed matter . . . not ordinarily assigned to the unit."

Last, it is *results-oriented*. It identifies the outcomes or outputs expected from the unit: "company correspondence," "publication materials."

How about your unit? Does it have a well-defined mission statement? In order to clearly understand the span of your responsibilities and range of your authority, you should have one. Then, you'll also have a sound basis for deciding what to delegate and to whom.

If your unit has a written mission statement, compare it with the structure just outlined: action-oriented, specific, and results-oriented. If you don't have a mission statement, formulate one, using the format outlined. If you're not sure of how it should read, check with your boss before writing it.

The goal statement summarizes all of Roxanne's responsibilities, since a manager's responsibilities and authority usually flow from the goal statement. Hers are outlined in the T-chart shown in Exhibit 2. The chart separates her supervisory responsibilities from her mission tasks.

When you read the chart, notice these four points:

1. All the items in the lists flow from the mission statement.
2. The list under supervisory responsibilities refers to what Roxanne does to help the unit meet its mission objectives; the opposite column lists what she, herself, does to meet those objectives.
3. The numbers in parentheses measure the hours per week she spends handling each responsibility (untimed items are periodic rather than weekly activities).
4. If Roxanne works as many hours a week as she says, she puts in eleven *hours* overtime each week.

After reading the chart, make a T-chart for yourself by listing supervisory responsibilities on the left-hand side and your line responsibilities (ordinary work of the unit that you do personally) on the right-hand side. When you're finished, compare your duties with your work group's mission statement.

You may want to show the T-chart to your boss and explain what you're trying to do, discussing each item in your list. Decide which of your line and/or supervisory duties it's in your power to delegate.

Whether or not you discuss the chart with your boss, answer these questions (and others that might come to mind):

1. Which of these items do in fact lie in the span of my responsibility and range of authority? If any of

Exhibit 2. Supervisory responsibilities vs. mission work.

Supervisory Responsibilities	Line Responsibilities*
• Maintain proper level of staffing to get the work done. • Distribute work (3).† • Monitor production rate and quality (3). • Act as liaison with other departments (2). • Maintain discipline of department. • Create unit production standards. • Complete daily, weekly, monthly, and quarterly production reports (3). • Write performance evaluations and conduct evaluation interviews. • Conduct periodic performance reviews with each employee. • Coach and counsel (5). • Attend meetings of committees producing work for unit (3). • Attend general management meetings. • Hold meetings with line employees to review progress, report company information, hear complaints, etc. (1). • Order supplies (1).	• Key in correspondence; same standard as word processors (5). • Key in training manual materials; same standard (15). • Proofread rate-manual materials (2). • Proofread all correspondence to maintain quality of work (8). • Help collate finished products (2).

*Mainly in late evenings
†Number of hours per week

Total hours: 51

13

them lie outside my span and range, why am I doing them?

2. How much of the authority that I'd like to delegate does company policy and practice permit my employees to assume?

3. Which of these responsibilities can I delegate? For what reasons will I delegate them?

4. Which of these responsibilities can I not delegate? Why not?

5. What are my accountabilities when I delegate tasks?

When you've answered these questions, you're almost ready to delegate work to your employees.

Chapter 3

The Benefits of Delegation and How You Keep Yourself From Enjoying Them

Almost ready, but not quite. You still have a great number of decisions to make, starting with two questions to ask about the value of delegating work.

1. Who might benefit from my delegating these responsibilities and how?
2. How would the group benefit from my delegating these responsibilities?

Answer the questions for yourself, if you can, before going on to see how we answer them.

Let's begin with how you'll benefit.

You, like Roxanne, probably perform crucial daily activities that impede your own productivity as a manager. By delegating some of that work, you *relieve yourself* of them. They get done, as they're supposed to, but you save your own time and energy for managerial duties.

At the same time, you assure yourself that the work gets done *properly*. You assign the task to the most appropriate person for the job—either because that person's ready to accept that responsibility and can learn how to do it or because he or she has expertise you lack.

When you delegate, you bring more hands and minds to bear on the problems of the work. That helps expedite decision making. By spreading decision making around the group, you and the group make more effective decisions.

You can use delegation as a tool for improving the

skills of your employees. You help them become more productive individuals and help them prepare for more technical jobs or for supervision. Since developing people is a supervisory responsibility, the more successful you are at this, the more recognition you'll get for it.

You not only improve individual productivity when you train and cross-train through delegating, you increase unit productivity as well. People can fill in for one another when someone's absent; people can help each other during peak periods; and they all can simply do more work.

Delegation helps you become the leader of the work group, not its "boss." People participating fully in group activities make important contributions—usually on their own initiative. They feel as if they're working with you, not for you. They admire and respect you and do what you want more willingly than if you boss them around.

The unit cohesion and effectiveness produce noticeable success, which enhances your prestige and influence in the organization. When you make your move to rise to the top (in your present organization or elsewhere), you have that success to buoy you.

But you're not the only beneficiary of delegation's largess. The organization as a whole and the people to whom you delegate tasks also benefit.

We can make short shrift of the organization's benefits: more productive people, more productivity, improved morale, improved communication and teamwork, greater profitability. Again, your prestige is greatly enhanced by the contribution you make to the organization's success.

It's more important, here, that you see how delegation affects the people you supervise because understanding the benefits to other people allows you to emphasize them when delegating tasks. The benefits supply the incentives you use for reinforcing motivation.

The people to whom you delegate personally benefit in at least three ways: They become more productive and valuable to the organization; the more valuable they feel, the more job satisfaction they experience; self-esteem improves as well. Sometimes personal satisfaction means as much as money.

Although not always, money rewards. Asking people to take on new and different tasks to help you and the organization becomes a possible means for receiving bonuses, raises, or some other tangible recognition. That's a matter of policy, however, and unless your organization specifically allows you to extend this offer to people willing to accept delegated tasks, don't do it.

Even if you can't promise a tangible reward such as money, by delegating work, you give people a way to learn new skills that they can trade on for a promotion, a raise, a transfer, or a job outside the company.

Not only do people who assume delegated tasks become more valuable to the organization, they also expand their importance to and influence on the work group. They become resources for people who need their help, and can function as backups for people in need of time off or who have too much to do. If you delegate some of your routine tasks to them, they become knowledgeable and skilled at handling some of the details and problems of running a work unit. One or two becomes, especially in your absence, a "lead person."

Finally, let's not overlook a basic need that some people feel is important: increasing knowledge or skill for its own sake. Some people just like to learn how to do new things, and they'll do it even you don't offer a tangible reward.

You wouldn't want to take advantage of someone, to be sure, because it doesn't take long for people to recognize when they are being used. So let people volunteer for anything they want to do, and they will. Just take care not to let them overload themselves or take on work that interferes with their ordinary duties.

Most people understand the benefits to themselves when you delegate work to them. Studies indicate that most employees wish their supervisors would delegate *more* work to them than they do. They want more responsibility, and they want the opportunity to grow and develop.

Supervisors as Their Own Worst Enemies

Many supervisors tend to create the barriers that come between them and delegating work. In her lament, Roxanne identified some of the barriers supervisors create for themselves: They prefer line work to shuffling paper; they think that no one can do the work better than they can; they feel a strong need to work at tasks with which they are most familiar; some feel threatened by the possibility that someone else might fail to complete a task for which upper management would hold them accountable.

Two other important barriers often stand in a supervisor's way: fear of losing power and improper planning. Let's take the fear first.

Fear of Losing Power

Some supervisors irrationally assume that by delegating work, they open the way for employees to take control of the unit, the unit will run itself without them, or, worse, the employees will then take control over them. "If I don't supervise them, they'll supervise me." Somehow people doing delegated jobs well suggests a usurpation of power, a *coup*.

There's nothing rational about such fears. These supervisors just don't want their employees to look better than they do or "show them up." They think upper management will see it and replace them.

But that's only the stuff out of which novels about corporate life are built. In real life, it's rare for employees to take over a department just because they perform delegated jobs well. In fact, management more commonly responds by rewarding the employee for a delegated job well-done *and* rewarding the supervisor for having the good sense to delegate the task to the employee.

If you think you suffer from Roxanne's "Delegation Blues," then reread the benefits to you and to the employees from delegating. The benefits alone should help you set aside any fears or worries you have that delegating can somehow do you in. If you feel good about the delegation and the person to whom you're delegating the job, and if you communicate those benefits to him or her, you'll get an enthusiastic response.

Roxanne is now convinced, as is evidenced by the following dialogue in which Roxanne asks Roger to help with some of her work, such as the daily, weekly, monthly, and quarterly production reports. He's one of the people who complete their almost error-free work in a timely manner.

They've been in a conference for a few minutes, passing some of the news of the day back and forth.

Roxanne: So, I've asked you come in for us to talk about a problem you might help me with if you're willing.

Roger: I'm willing to listen, anyway. What's up?

Roxanne: I've looked at my own situation, my workload, and to tell the truth, I'm my own worst enemy.

Roger: Meaning?

Roxanne: I've taken on much more than I can possibly do in a day, and, in the process, I haven't been exactly fair to you or to anyone else. As a result, I haven't left the office before 7 P.M. in ages, and you people haven't been given much chance to learn how to do new or different things, or to grow into new jobs.

Roger: You're saying, then, you'd like me to help you.

Roxanne: There's no sense in kidding myself or you. I need the help, and until now I've been—well—afraid to ask for it. The reasons aren't important. Attribute it to false pride and let it go at that.

Roger:	Fine with me.
Roxanne:	Roger, I've hurt myself as well as the rest of you by not trusting you to do the things I've been doing for so long—like producing the training manuals or putting together reports.
Roger:	[*Semi-joking, nervous*] Is this true confessions, or what? I'm not sure I understand.
Roxanne:	[*Laughing, also nervous*] It's not easy to admit I've made these mistakes, but I have made them, and I'm admitting it. I need the help, and you and the others need a way into the territory I roped off for myself—things you feel you can and want to do.
Roger:	I guess the flip answer is, Hey, I like it this way; you do all the hard stuff, you get to stay late while I get to go home; why should I give up all that?
Roxanne:	Do you really mean it?
Roger:	No, I understand. Some of my doubt comes from thinking you'd never do this on your own. Sure, I'd like to learn to do more than key in correspondence. It's boring. Sure, I want to grow into new jobs. I don't want to sit in front of that screen the rest of my life. And you're right, I would like you to trust me to do the work.

Still, positive attitudes and enthusiasm won't cure all the "Delegation Blues" you may have. Improper planning and employee-created barriers can undermine the best of intentions.

Improper Planning

Even supervisors with no fear of delegating sometimes shoot themselves in the foot through improper planning. They delegate the wrong jobs—personal chores or work they find distasteful—or delegate important work to people incapable of learning the task or unwilling to do it.

Sometimes they fail to set deadlines or explain the task's objectives. They don't transfer authority as well as responsibility. Or they fail to take into account the person's or the organization's needs and requirements. They don't do the things you'll do after reading this book.

While learning the ropes that surround delegating, Roxanne is making plenty of mistakes:

Roxanne: It's been a week since you began working on the 2630. Getting the hang of it?

Val: More or less.

Roxanne: I was looking over some of your work on it, and most of it looks pretty good—a few errors here and there. But, you're not getting out very much work yet.

Val: Well, how much should I be getting out? I didn't know I had any production goals on that machine. After all, I'm just getting used to it.

Roxanne: I don't think there's any reason to get upset. You should be getting out almost as much as you do on the other equipment.

Val: Why didn't you say so when we started on this project? I don't think I can do that. This is a much more complex piece than anything I've ever operated, and I don't think I can get back up to speed that quickly. You're not being fair.

Roxanne didn't take into account two main issues. One, when people learn a new task—or, in this case, how to operate a new piece of equipment—they concentrate first on quality, then on quantity. It's a function of the learning curve. Two, she hadn't set a production standard at the *start* of the project: a realistic, achievable standard with which Val could have agreed.

By not doing those things, she ran into what many supervisors experience: the barriers employees can create.

Chapter 4

Employee-Created Barriers to Delegation and How to Counter Them

Not only do supervisors create barriers, the people to whom they want to delegate erect them too. Hurdles are so prevalent, they have names: *imposition; ignorance; stagnation; fear; eagerness; group pressure;* and *power playing*.

Imposition

Supervisors often inadvertently collaborate with their employees in setting up obstacles, as in one form of imposition. Since supervisors look to their best people for help, they often ask for it at about the same time the employee has done something noteworthy.

Roxanne: Since you did that report so well, I'm think-
ing— Why don't you do this too?

Sue: C'mon. Why push it off on me just because I did my job well?"

With poor timing and insensitive wording, Roxanne created one barrier. The employee produced the second one.

Sue feels imposed upon or punished for doing well. She rejects the additional work and could very well reject any delegated task thereafter, believing that any delegation is itself a form of punishment.

Your employees may believe you're imposing on them, passing off your own work, or taking advantage of their good nature even if you don't do anything like

---

Employee-Created Barriers

1. Imposition
2. Ignorance
3. Stagnation

4. Fear of failure
   or of peers
5. Eagerness
6. Power playing

---

what Roxanne did. In this instance, they may not have a clear picture of your managerial role and how much more of that work you could do if you delegated mission tasks to them. Usually a frank discussion of how you'll be more productive or available for other assignments, coupled with a clear statement of the advantage to the other person, is enough to overcome this resistance.

Ignorance

Some people erect the ignorance barrier because they don't understand that they always need new skills to get some of the things they want. In all likelihood, you may have to help an employee identify some unattained goal to which learning how to do the additional work would contribute. For example, telling the employee that he or she could be passed over for promotion might do the trick—*if* that's important to that person.

Here Roxanne talks with Val:*

Roxanne: Is this what you want to do always?
Val: [*Flippantly*] It's a living.
Roxanne: I guess so. But, Val, isn't there anything else you want out of your career?
Val: [*Still flippant*] A job is *not* a career. I'm making out.
Roxanne: That's not the Val I know. You read sci-

*This and a variety of other dialogues are adapted from Donald H. Weiss, *Successful Delegation,* a cassette/workbook program produced by the American Management Association's Extension Institute (Watertown, Mass.: 1987).

	ence fiction, you go to the symphony, collect prints. Sitting in front of a screen doesn't fit that.
Val:	[*A little more serious*] I suppose you're right. But, I do the work better than anyone else here—what *I* understand the work to be. I get along with everyone, and they'll work for me. That's what I thought it took to get your job or one like it somewhere else.
Roxanne:	Getting ahead here, or anywhere else, takes more than doing the work. Handling people's important, but supervision goes beyond the work and the people. It includes everything else that goes on here. Collecting those data and preparing those reports will give you experience with management control materials. And a leg up on other people.
Val:	I see that now. And I really do want more for myself than just sitting at a machine all day.

Fiction may *mirror* reality, but reality doesn't always move that easily. It could happen that a Val would *not want* more for herself than doing the work and collecting a paycheck, as you'll see under the next heading, stagnation. Sometimes it's easier to move someone if you know what incentives to use to get the response you want. But that's grist for another book in the Successful Office Skills series: *How to Get the Best from Other People.*

Stagnation

Although stagnation resembles ignorance and a fear of failure (which we'll discuss later), they differ. Ignorance or fear can produce stagnation, but usually neither is involved.

Some people don't want to change. They're in their own niche and want to stay there. Here's another version of how Val could have answered Roxanne.

Roxanne: Sitting in front of a PC all day doesn't strike me as the Val I know.

Val: *[Flippantly]* That's really it. Do my job, take my pay, go home. My real life's there—with my kids. I do this for extra money. No need to become a bigshot around here or anywhere else.

That attitude, in this version of the story, doesn't make Val a poor employee unless she rebels against and resists the growth and development of the group as a whole. She resides within a comfort zone that suits her.

People like *this* Val usually just want to be left alone. They're the good soldiers who do what they have to as long as they're out of the limelight, away from public notice, and performing jobs that can be done quickly and safely.

Fear

Just as fear immobilizes many supervisors, many employees reject new tasks out of fear. It's not just the task that frightens them. Some fear failure and others fear their coworkers will see them as "the favorite" or "boss's pet" if they take on extra work.

Here's an illustration of the fear of failure and how to handle it:

Roger: *[Disturbed]* I can't do that. You're asking me to learn a whole new program on a PC. I don't think I can master that one. It's awfully complicated.

Val: But I need your help. I'm overloaded right now because of that New York claim. You know how large it is.

Roxanne: I know you can do it, and Val needs the help.

Roger: What if I blow it? Blow it, and I look bad.

Roxanne: I understand your concern, but I've confidence in you. I've seen you do this sort of thing before. As for botching the job, any

	of us can do that. That's a risk we all take, but I don't think you'll blow it. Besides, I'll be around to help you.
Val:	So will I. Just ask whenever you have a question or a problem.
Roger:	[*Reluctantly*] Okay, but I think this one'll do me in.

By recognizing that Roger's fears are unrealistic—he's a quick study and learns well—Roxanne allays them, as does Val. Roger will do the job and do it well.

People often fear imaginary conditions, and to them the unreal is as real as anything else, as when people think that by taking on a delegated task the group will turn on them or that everyone's attitudes toward them will change. Ordinarily that's not the case. Most frequently, the attitude is one of—

Roger: *Poor you!* Roxanne's always finding extra work for *you* to do.

Other times it's one of—

Val: *Lucky you!* You get to do that interesting stuff. Well, maybe when I get caught up, I can do some of that, too.

I'm not saying that peer pressure never interferes with delegation. It often does, and some people buckle under that pressure: They conform; they refuse to do any extra work.

When the problem is imaginary—fear of pressure that really doesn't exist or fear of failure when its possibility is slight—you can usually help people confront their fear, help them get past it the way Roxanne and Val did with Roger. But, don't try to play psychologist in the process. Deal with the issues and problems related to the job, not with the whys and wherefores of the fear.

Unless the fear is truly neurotic, you should be able to handle the problem. If it is neurotic—if the person's fear seems repetitive, inappropriate, and incapacitating—encourage him or her to recognize it and get the proper professional help.

When the group pressure is genuine, uncover its source. It could emanate from only one person or it could come from a group attitude or from your organization's culture. Whatever the source, talk with the people responsible. Demonstrate the problems their pressure creates for themselves as well as for the organization. You have to deal with it before you can expect any one person to defy his or her peers.

Eagerness

Although you don't want to stifle enthusiasm, be aware of problems created by *too much* enthusiasm. In addition to becoming overloaded, some people are too willing to take on tasks for which they may not be ready. Eager to please, with a need for social recognition, they jump out ahead of themselves, very often bungling the job in the attempt.

Just as you need the good soldiers, you also need these eager beavers; but you need to move them more slowly than they want to go, while nurturing their enthusiasm. Bring them along slowly and carefully, assigning tasks to them in relation to their abilities to get them done successfully.

Power Playing

Sometimes eagerness masks a more difficult barrier to overcome: a power play. Power players accept additional tasks only under conditions unduly favorable to themselves. Instead of feeling that you're imposing on them, these people see the acceptance of a delegated task as an opportunity to take advantage of you and literally blackmail you.

Had he not been afraid of the new task he was assigned, Roger could have taken Roxanne aside and said:

Roger: [*Conspiratorily*] I wanted to talk to you alone because I didn't want to say this in front of Val. Look. I need an extra dollar

	an hour. I can't make it on less. If I do that job for Val, I'll expect that raise.
Roxanne:	I understand your need for a raise. Everyone can use more money. You also seem to understand the need for getting this work done.
	Now, I can't promise you a raise. Not till the budget is cleared for the next quarter; you know that. I'll note your help in your performance management file and enter it into your appraisal. We can make a case later in the year for increasing your pay.
	You know, there's something else to consider here, too. How do you think Val feels about getting your help?
Roger:	I suppose she's pretty grateful.
Roxanne:	Probably. How do you think that gratitude will affect you?
Roger:	I get your drift. She'll probably scratch my back someday, too.
Roxanne:	That's exactly my drift. But, Roger. There's one last thing I want you to think about. I'd appreciate it if you don't try this kind of power play again, because if you do, instead of a commendation, I'll enter a reprimand into your file.

Roxanne makes it clear that organizational policy limits rewards or makes them commensurate with the importance, gravity, or difficulty of the task. By making the limits perfectly clear—including the negative consequences of game playing—she also controls the power player.

In Conclusion

Steps can be taken to overcome the barriers. Explaining the advantages of the delegation frequently solves the problem. Otherwise, take the various steps we've discussed in this chapter.

Chapter 5

The Proactive Manager's Guide to Planning the Delegation Process

If you don't already know what "proactive" means, you'll figure it out from this: It's *the opposite of* "reactive." Instead of reacting to problems, proactive managers try to anticipate them, prevent them, or, if not, head them off and then prevent them from becoming crises. Proactive delegation means planning the delegation process itself, as well as the job being delegated.

Managers who delegate work effectively take pains to plan the process carefully. When planning to delegate work, they think through three key aspects of the process: organizational demands and customs; the demands of forecasting workloads; and available resources.

Organizational Demands and Customs

If you haven't done much delegating before, you must start from scratch—not something to do by yourself. Bring in your supervisor again to discuss the limits of your authority to delegate certain tasks. Find out what responsibilities your policies and customs permit you to delegate (and what they don't). That way you avoid barriers erected by the *formal* organization.

At the same time, check out the limits of authority you can assign. Some organizations allow people to delegate the work but insist that if something comes up that requires an independent judgment or decision,

---

1. Consider organizational demands and customs.
2. Forecast workloads.
3. Be aware of human and material resources.
4. Make rational decisions.

---

the supervisor has to answer the question. For example, Roxanne can delegate the preparation of production reports to Val, but she can't give to the employee her discretion to modify the production standards involved.

During the discussion with your supervisor, determine where your employee's accountability ends and yours begins. Since delegation means "to transfer responsibilities and authority to someone else," you also have to transfer accountability. The employee has to know what's expected and how the results will be evaluated. You buy a bag of trouble unless you spell out all three—the responsibilities, the authority, and the accountabilities.

But, they're yours to begin with. While you can give away a responsibility completely, you *don't want* to abrogate your authority over it, and the organization will not let you abandon your accountability. The employee has to perform the activities and achieve the objectives, but you're responsible for seeing to it that the work gets done properly and on time. In essence, when the employee does well, you say:

Roxanne: Roger did a great job, even though he thought at first he couldn't do it at all.

When he or she "blows it," you say:

Roxanne: *We* gave it our best shot, but somewhere along the way *I missed* the signs that problems were brewing.

Of course, if the employee can't seem to get the hang of doing the delegated task, you take it away and give it to someone else.

30

One demand some *formal* organizations make concerns union contracts. Where they exist, you have to check on what you can and can't delegate and to whom. The contract governs the work rules.

On the other hand, in many places, the *informal* organization—customs—also governs work rules. It could be that traditionally some jobs are delegated only to specific people. If such a custom exists where you are, assign those jobs to someone else at your own risk, possibly offending the traditions and the people who live by them. Check out your organization's culture before you make decisions on your own.

Forecasting Work

You're also best-advised not to try to project your unit's workload without discussing it with your supervisor and with supervisors in interconnected areas. *Guesstimating* doesn't cut it, "Well, last year we did so much, so this year we'll increase it by 10 percent."

If your organization doesn't plan interdepartmental workflows in a group process, meet individually with each supervisor of an area that affects your area's work. Include support groups, such as word processing (which may or may not be able handle the work flowing from your area), as well as areas that pass through work to you.

Get those groups to give you a realistic estimate of the magnitude of their effect on your area during the coming year (or part thereof). Badger them if you have to, but get that information before you start people on new or different jobs. These projections may even enable you to decide what new delegated tasks to assign.

Control over timing falls out from projecting workflow, and timing is an important factor in planning. Waiting for a crisis before assigning work defeats the purposes of effective delegation. Effective delegators prevent problems from becoming crises by proactively assigning work at appropriate times for the unit and for the people to whom the work is given.

Available Resources

In order to delegate work appropriately, proactive managers need to get to know their employees. It's through them that the work gets done, and supervisors should identify the human factors that move the process efficiently.

Working through Personnel or on their own, they develop a talent skill bank. They have some idea of what their employees can do *in addition* to the work for which they were hired. Aptitudes hide everywhere: in previous jobs, in hobbies, in interests, and in leisure-time pursuits. Wise supervisors keep a sharp eye out for the unexpected resource and tap it when they need it.

They also find out their employee's interests, wishes, and aspirations. Just because a person has skills, it doesn't follow that he or she wants to apply them. Past jobs, for example: A person may not want to dredge them up again. They also may not fit his or her present wants; having to do "old stuff" may be demeaning to the person.

Tapping into aspirations may produce more effective results. Learning new skills usually excites and challenges employees more than does dredging out old ones. Knowing what your employees want for themselves— what turns them on—gives you the data you need for deciding to whom to assign what. Remember how Roxanne handled Val?

Roxanne: That's not the Val I know. You read science fiction, you go to the symphony, collect prints. Sitting in front of a screen doesn't fit that.

Once you've determined your authorities, limits, and accountabilities—once you've done your homework about the organization and your employees—you're ready to plan the delegation itself.

Rational Decision Making

Effective delegators still *sometimes* stand alone when they decide what to delegate, to whom, and when.

Especially if the delegation is a training exercise, they outline all the steps and identify the resources and the possible barriers. They pinpoint the possible problems and devise several alternative solutions. They then hand the entire plan to the employee.

On *most* other occasions, they involve the person to whom the work is delegated in the planning process, making the shift of responsibility easier and producing a real commitment to the task. They also involve the group in the planning process when it's appropriate. The situation determines the best method of making the decision.

The following questions will help you decide what to delegate and whom to involve in making decisions. Instead of just reading them, answer them and make decisions about delegating some of your own work to someone. Evaluate to whom and how to delegate responsibilities you listed in the T-chart modeled after the one shown in Exhibit 2, and which you discussed with your boss.

I've listed ten questions that will help you decide to whom to delegate a task. Add any similar questions you have to answer that may have been left out.

When you've finished answering these questions, you'll have a list of people to whom you can delegate tasks. Hold on to it. Don't rush off to turn the work over to them yet. Before you do that, you'll want to answer this question: *How will delegating this work to a particular person benefit both the unit and the person?* In a bit, I'll be talking about how best to communicate the answer to that question.

To Whom Should Responsibilities Be Delegated?

Use the following questions for each task you intend to delegate. Make sure you've covered each question for every item on your list and for each person you intend to involve.

Ideally, for complete coverage, use a separate piece of paper for each task. Name each person you believe capable of doing it or capable of learning how to do it. Then answer these questions:

1. Who has the experience and/or training to do this job without additional training?
2. Who can get the job done the quickest and with the least amount of training?
3. Who has the time to do the job and/or learn to do it in addition to his/her current workload?
4. On whom would assigning this task have the worst impact with respect to current workload, etc.?
5. Which person doing this task would make the greatest contribution to the unit's efforts?
6. Who would benefit the most from doing this work?
7. Who would make the least contribution to the unit by doing this work (that is, other work would suffer or it wouldn't make much difference to the unit if a specific person did the work)?
8. Who would benefit the least from doing this work?
9. If I assign this work to someone in the group, on which other person or people would the delegation have the worst impact?
10. If I assign this work to someone in the group, on which other person or people (other than myself) would the delegation have the best effects?

In Conclusion

When planning to delegate work, take into account everything and anything that could affect the effectiveness of the delegation. Since you're trying to increase efficiencies and productivity, you don't want to overlook something that could interfere with your or the employee doing the work. Now, how you communicate the plan can be one of the worst obstacles to effective delegation.

Chapter 6

Communicating the Delegation: A Four-Step Plan

Once you decide how to make your delegation decision and to whom to delegate the task, you're ready to do it. Now comes the most difficult part: telling the other person what you want (what you expect him or her to accomplish), why you want it, and what he or she will gain from doing it. Well-planned, effective communication makes for effective delegation.

What You Want

The other person can't read your mind, and you don't know how well he or she interprets what you're saying. Since it's your show, you have the responsibility of making your wants clear and unambiguous.

It's best to write down the results you want (the job's objectives) and the standards by which you'll judge the results. Writing them down gives you the chance to describe the task and its standards as precisely as possible.

Seven criteria guide writing a task's objectives and standards:

1. The targets should refer to measurable or observable actions.
2. The tasks should have deadlines by when certain things are done.
3. The objectives should outline the means and conditions by which the person will accomplish the task.
4. They should be realistic and achievable.

5. They should be specific, yet open to revision.
6. They should include provisions for monitoring and reviewing the work.
7. They should spell out the positive consequences of doing the job well and the negative consequences of not so doing—consequences for the individual, for the unit, and for the organization as a whole.

Meeting these criteria for writing objectives and standards reduces the risk of misunderstanding—yet another barrier to effective delegation.

Why You Want to Delegate

Since this is your agenda, you have to make it clear to the other person why shifting responsibility to him or her is important—to you, to him or her, to the unit, and to the organization.

Tie the doing of the task to the unit's work objectives and the organization's business objectives. Business objectives drive any organization, even not-for-profits. They're the reasons for which the organization exists. Truthfully, not all organizations have written out a business plan, and many that have written one don't always follow it; nevertheless, the doing of any kind of business is goal-directed rather than random.

Well-designed, thoughtful business plans outline objectives that meet the needs of four constituencies: the consumers, the society, the organization as a whole, and the individual employee. Any unit and every job in the organization will meet the needs of at least one of those groups, often more than one. Satisfying those needs constitute the objectives. When delegating a job, you must describe how it satisfies a business need.

Roxanne: I understand when you say you don't know why we need to produce these production reports every day.

Sue: They cut into our production time.

Roxanne: Still, we have to produce them for upper

management. They use them to project manpower needs. Our current growth outstrips our ability to meet the policyholders' needs. We have to see just where we need to add people to keep up with work so we can try to get ahead of it.

If you're using delegation to cross-train, explain how cross-training satisfies group needs, e.g., backup, support, mutual assistance. Be specific and open to questions.

More important than why *you* want this to happen, the person should understand what he or she stands to gain from doing it.

What the Employee Stands to Gain

Decide in advance of your meeting with the employee which of the benefits discussed in Chapter 3 is likely to be of value to that person. Personalize each one. Identify some type of payoff—a reward—that you think this person would get from doing it.

It doesn't have to be monetary. It could be something as simple as an afternoon off or as complicated as personal satisfaction.

People come to work motivated. Why else would they come to work for you? Sometimes, people come to work for a particular firm or a specific unit because it's all they can get—they're there whether they want to be or not—but they're the exception, not the rule.

Motivation comes from within the person, and people are motivated to satisfy both work-related and personal needs and interests. Another book in this series, *Managing Stress** contains a self-evaluation called, What Drives You? It helps identify what you believe are your most important payoffs, or "drivers."

You may want to complete that evaluation for yourself, and if you feel it does you some good, you could ask your employees to complete it also. Discuss it

*Donald H. Weiss (AMACOM, 1987).

together. It could help you provide the incentives that will maintain your employees' motivation.

Motivation on the job becomes a problem when people feel the organization rides over their needs or frustrates their interests. You can see to it that your employees' motivation survives the daily grind by reconciling organizational and employee aims. You'll not be able to do that unless you know something about what makes a reward valuable to any one specific person.

Your employees expect you to provide this kind of productive environment because you and your employees formed a psychological contract when they came to work. The psychological contract, almost always unwritten, sets up your expectations of each other.

The employees expect to satisfy their needs in return for their labors, and they expect you to help them do it. Unless the rewards you offer fit those needs, the person becomes demotivated, often quitting weeks— months—before they leave the organization.

Appropriate rewards reinforce the behavior for which the person is rewarded, and he or she remains motivated to do more and better than ever.

How You Say It

When you want someone to do something, the way in which you organize the discussion about the task can draw the employee into the planning or leave you giving instructions to an uncommitted drone. Another supervisor-created barrier consists of talking too much, not finding out, first of all, if the employee can do the job or wants to do it and not giving the person an opportunity to participate in planning the delegated task.

To help prevent that barrier, discuss the delegation using a patterned four-part method: (1) gatekeeping; (2) exchanging viewpoints; (3) resolving disagreements; (4) action planning.

Gatekeeping

As the name implies, gatekeeping opens the conversation. Since this is your agenda and the employee doesn't have any idea what it's about, you have to work at making the other person comfortable in the situation.

Talk in private. In an open-space environment, try to find a conference room in which to talk over the task.

On the way to the conference room, or as he or she takes a seat in your office, set the other person's possible concerns to rest with a friendly greeting and by briefly talking about unrelated matters: business chitchat; the latest profit figures; the new marketing plan—anything positive and upbeat. This way you show that the occasion's a friendly one. Then state the purpose of the meeting.

Once the person understands you want to talk about delegating some work to him or her, test the waters of interest with a simple question: "Sound interesting?" If the person says, "No," you can find out why. Turn the objection around, if you want to, by showing him or her the benefits of at least taking a closer look at the proposition.

When you both agree to talk further and have not so far used the four steps we're describing for holding this discussion, explain how you'd like to go about it. Exchange viewpoints, resolve any disagreements you might have, and set up an action plan. Even if the person's familiar with this way of conducting a meeting, it doesn't hurt to reinforce the fact that you're planning to stick by it.

Then you ask for the other person's commitment to working with you in this matter of a delegated task.

Another compressed dialogue helps illustrate the entire gatekeeping process:

Roxanne: [*As she and Roger enter the conference room*] What do you think of the new word processor?

Roger: I think it'll help a lot. It's state of the art. Does everything but key in its own data.

39

Roxanne:	I think so, too. The journals are raving about it. [*After a slight pause*] Roger, I'm going to need your help again. Upper management's asked us to track all the traffic coming through here. They want a summary of everything—not just the count we now make. Who, what, why, where, when—the works.
Roger:	Whatever for?
Roxanne:	They're talking about a second shift.
Roger:	Oh?
Roxanne:	It could mean a lot to us. Take off some of the pressure—create a new supervisor slot. Sound interesting?
Roger:	Well, yeah, but it sounds like a big job. I don't know if I can handle it.
Roxanne:	What concerns you?
Roger:	Time. I'm already pretty loaded up.
Roxanne:	You're concerned about the current work-load. How do you think we can get around that?
Roger:	I guess I can put in an extra hour a day to collect and summarize the log. Get here early if I can't stay late.
Roxanne:	That much overtime will do it, but do you really want to put in that much?
Roger:	If I have to.
Roxanne:	That's great, but why are you willing to do that?
Roger:	We'll need a shift supervisor, won't we?
Roxanne:	I can't promise that.
Roger:	I understand that. This isn't another power play. But, the way I see it, the person who does this report has a better than fair shot at the job.
Roxanne:	Could be. So, you're ready to get into it?
Roger:	What'll it take.
Roxanne:	I'd like some of your ideas on how to put it together before I make any suggestions. If we have any disagreement, we'll set it right before setting up a complete plan. Okay?

Roger: Gotcha.

Roxanne set the stage and has Roger solving the problems (e.g., time). Now, the gate is wide open and they can move on to the next step: exchanging viewpoints.

Exchanging Viewpoints

Listening to the other person's opinions or feelings before you express yours, letting the other person go first, keeps you from plunging into a situation filled with the dangers of unnecessary disagreement. While he or she's talking, clear your mind of everything else (including your possible responses).

Ask questions for clarification, indicating that you don't understand. When the person's finished, give a short summary of what he or she said to check out whether you fully grasped what he or she suggests or expresses. You're not communicating unless you both agree you do understand.

Giving a person the first shot gives you more than mutual understanding. It gives you commitment from the other person. Having done most of the planning, it's hard for someone to reject his or her own ideas and opinions. Play President and Congress: you propose; let the other person dispose.

Here's another snippet of dialogue:

Roger: So, I think we have each person complete their own log. I'll set up a new template that'll capture most of what we need as we log in the job.
Roxanne: You're saying you'll build it right into the machine log itself.
Roger: That's right.
Roxanne: I don't see how you'll do it.
Roger: It won't be easy, but if we took the log as it now works and . . . .

We'll "fade out" here and "fade back in" as Roxanne says:

Roxanne:	I think I see it. You want to have us each make the data entries necessary for listing and collating everything going into the machine. Then we print out each person's log on a daily basis. Is that it?
Roger:	Right.
Roxanne:	It sounds interesting. Anything else?
Roger:	Not that I can think of off the top of my head.
Roxanne:	I agree with most of it, but I don't know if we can produce the kind of template you're talking about without producing a mountain of paper every day. What do you think?

Although it's hard to show it in a brief space, Roxanne's applying the 20 percent rule: She's letting the employee do 80 percent of the talking. Now that she has a chance to chime in, she makes it short, concise, and to the point. She's ready to move into step 3: resolve disagreements.

Resolving Disagreements

Eliminating misunderstandings or resolving differences when they arise prevents them from becoming barriers later. You need to deal with each one immediately, before passing on to something else. Don't put off problem solving until the problem becomes a crisis.

Again, let the employee take the lead in working out a solution. You don't have to agree with everything suggested, but you do yourself a great favor by listening with an open mind. He or she will return the compliment.

Let's tune in on Roxanne and Roger again:

Roger:	I don't think that's a real problem.
Roxanne:	How come?
Roger:	After I key in the individual logs into the summary, I'll just chuck it all.
Roxanne:	That sounds like a duplication of effort.
Roger:	I think I see what you mean. They log in

their reports, I copy them. Sounds like we need a way to produce a consolidated log in one step. I got it. The new processor. I'll bet I can set up a template that takes it all and. . . .

Another fadeout at this point. The point's been made. A disagreement or misunderstanding is an opportunity for creative problem solving. Give your employees half a chance and they'll solve their own problems. In our story, Roger's already moving on to the last step: action planning.

Developing an Action Plan

Now you and the employee together set goals and objectives and standards of performance. You've already told the person what you want. The story's "want" is a summary report of all the traffic through the unit. With the action plan, you formally set out in writing the targets and deadlines for completing each step or part of the project and how well the job is to be done. This is also where you set the limits to the person's authority.

When you feel comfortable that this other person can make creative and effective, independent decisions, you can simply say, "Get it done. Bring it to me when you're finished." However, in most cases, *you'll* probably be more comfortable taking a consultative role. You might give this type of employee the following instruction:

Roxanne: Set it up. Give me several possibilities to discuss with you. You'll make the final decision, but I'd like to see what you're considering, first.

In other cases, especially if someone is learning how to do the job, you'll want to keep closer tabs on what he or she is doing. You'll want more frequent reports, and you'll want to make more of the plans and the decisions. It's a personal call as to how much authority you release to the other person.

Golden Rule of Problem Solving

Don't come to me with a problem unless
you also bring three alternative solutions.

Finally, through planning, you'll both look at the means and resources available for doing the job and those still needed. In short, the plan identifies all the conditions necessary for the successful completion of the task.

The conditions include obstacles to successful completion. So include contingency plans for dealing with potential problems. Also identify the role you'll play in the person's activities. Make specific and definite appointments for periodic progress checks.

To ensure that your plan is complete and that you both agree on what to expect from each other, write everything down. The format shown in Exhibit 3 gives you a way to pull the plan together. It provides space for writing out each aspect of the plan, but if you need more space for any one item, attach an extra page.

You can use that format as a short memo or you can use it as the basis for writing a more formal communication to the other person that tells him or her on what you've agreed: the plan. Then the question of what you agreed upon can't be debated in the event the job isn't done or is done improperly.

Practice using the format in the exhibit by completing it for any task of your own. Ask your supervisor to work on it with you if you think that it would be of value for you both.

In Conclusion

Using the four steps for talking over the task you want to delegate gives both you and the employee an opportunity to examine what has to be done. The other person will have a clear picture of what he or she needs to do, and you'll find out if the person's ready to

Exhibit 3. Action plan.

Name _____

Task _____

OBJECTIVE [*Include target, deadlines*]:

MEANS AND STEPS [*Include most important available resources and those still needed as well as most important activities*]:

CONTINGENCIES [*Include all the things you think could go wrong and ways to deal with them*]:

SUPERVISOR'S RESPONSIBILITIES [*Include what you can do to help and how you will monitor progress*]:

MEASURES [*Include standards and results you will use to judge when the job is done and how well it has been done*]:

CHECKPOINTS [*Include appointments to review progress*]:

do it. If not, you'll have to find ways to train him or her. If the employee is reluctant to do the task, you'll have to find ways to encourage him or her to take it on, unless it isn't worth it to you to pursue delegating the task to that person.

Once the task is delegated, your main duty is to monitor progress and lend assistance when it's needed.

Chapter 7

Keeping Your Eye on Things: How to Make Sure Delegated Work Is Done—And Done Well

Even when you leave the person alone to perform a delegated task, the success of the project depends largely on how you apply management controls. That's what we mean by *monitoring.*

The supervisor always bears ultimate accountability for any delegated task. Remember, upper management assigns tasks to the supervisor, not to his or her employees. That he or she chooses to delegate is that person's decision—*and responsibility.* Guess to whom upper management will come when it wants the finished product—to the employee or to the supervisor?

Additionally, the supervisor is responsible for the quality standards and deadlines of any work coming through the unit. No manager can afford to turn an employee completely loose on a project. To ensure that he or she fulfills the managerial responsibilities of the supervisory role, a supervisor has to give adequate and proportionate attention to the people to whom he or she assigns work. If an employee is learning the job or performing a task for the first time, the supervisor may have to lend a greater proportion of energy to that person than to other employees.

That's why a supervisor has to learn how much control to exert: when to take no further action or when to reserve final judgments. He or she needs to know when to back off competent people and when to step in appropriately. Effectively designed monitoring devices will help you decide when to step in and when to lay back.

Proactive managers rarely look over their trained or experienced employees' shoulders. They sit back and monitor delegated work by asking for periodic reports or conferences. They use monitoring tools for giving feedback and solving problems.

By reviewing procedures and reports, they can give appropriate feedback that helps the person stay on track or make corrections if deviations begin appearing. They also use the information collected to coach the people who make mistakes or who need additional training. At times, they use those tools for giving or withholding rewards, depending on how the work is done.

When problems begin to surface, especially those neither the supervisor nor the employee had anticipatged when they began planning a task, the proactive manager realizes that blaming the person or putting him or her "in his (her) place" won't make the problems go away. Instead, they use the four-step method to help solve those problems—in the same way they used it when planning the job. Together they identify the causes of the problems and plan steps for overcoming them. If it turns out that the person deliberately failed, then appropriate negative (disciplinary) action can be taken.

The action plan I discussed earlier provides you with the written goals, job standards, and schedules that help guide the employee and you. When you have a written plan, you know what to watch for, and by watching for deviations you can act proactively to prevent problems from becoming crises.

In sum, the successful completion of a delegated task is as much the supervisor's concern as it is that of the employee to whom the task is delegated. Keeping an eye on things is to everyone's best interest.

Conclusion

In the beginning of this book I said you'd be in a better position to delegate effectively than Roxanne was when you met her. You should now feel more comfortable assigning work you might have done yourself to someone else. Rather than merely unloading responsibilities on other people, you should be able to use delegation as a *management* tool for helping you lead your work team toward achieving its objectives while meeting your own objectives and those of the organization—and helping your employees to grow.

Delegation, in short, is one of those effective uses of human resources that describe management. If you're not getting the maximum positive results from the people who report to you, you have to learn the same hard lesson Roxanne learned: how to give away *non*supervisory work and how to get help from other people.

"Getting positive results" means seeing to it that your unit accomplishes *its* objectives. That's a supervisory objective, not a mission objective.

Supervisory objectives involve achieving those results by hiring, training, coaching, counseling, and directing other people; by planning, problem solving, monitoring, taking corrective action, and rewarding for success. None of those activities is possible unless you can delegate. A supervisor produces the best results by *not* doing the unit's work but rather by doing his or her management job.

Index

About the Author

Donald H. Weiss, Ph.D., of Millers' Mutual Insurance in Alton, Illinois, has been engaged in education and training for over twenty-six years and has written numerous articles, books, audiocassette/workbook programs, and video training films on effective sales and supervisory or management skills. He speaks regularly on stress management and other personal development subjects, and has produced a variety of related printed or recorded materials.

During his career, Dr. Weiss has been the Manager of Special Projects for a training and development firm, the Manager of Management Training for an insurance company, the Director of Training for an employment agency group, a training consultant, and a writer-producer-director of video training tapes. He also has taught at several universities and colleges in Texas, including the University of Texas at Arlington and Texas Christian University in Fort Worth.

Currently, Dr. Weiss is Corporate Training Director for Millers' Mutual Insurance.